Hi Ruth,

I seem to have acquired 2 of this booklet — wondered if you might be interested? — or pass it on to someone else your end — written by a URC guy!!

Lots of love
Liz

The Christmas Stories in Faith and Preaching

John Proctor
Director of New Testament Studies
Westminster College, Cambridge

GROVE BOOKS LIMITED
RIDLEY HALL RD   CAMBRIDGE   CB3 9HU

Contents

Preface

Material in this book has been shared in various parts and forms, over a number of years, with students in the Cambridge Theological Federation, with URC Ministers in Suffolk, and with Baptist Lay Preachers in Cambridgeshire. I am grateful for their questions and comments. I learned much from them, and hope that this learning process was not entirely one-sided.

Plenty of ideas in these pages have come from other people's books. Some of the debts are acknowledged in footnotes. The scope of a Grove booklet, and my inability to recall the source of every thought, mean that the list is surely incomplete. I apologize if there are significant omissions.

The Cover Illustration is by Peter Ashton

First Impression September 1998
Reprinted September 2008
ISSN 1365-490X
ISBN 978 1 85174 382 7

Introduction

Shepherds and a star, wise men at the manger, oxen and asses gazing at the child, and winter's snow on the ground outside—the Christmas story has itself a kind of snowball capacity.

It all gets gathered and squeezed together, and picks up a good deal of material that did not originally belong to it. Yet it commands a strange fascination. People recognize it, and love it. It has a popular appeal that seems to be matched by little else in our Christian story. From one point of view Christmas is a strong card in our hand, a good opportunity to celebrate and share our faith with a wider selection of our neighbours than are usually interested.

From another standpoint Christmas can be awkward to handle. The season itself is so overlaid with sentiment that when the moment passes, the mood fades too, and any message it carried is quickly forgotten. If we are not careful the Bible stories themselves may become part of the sentimentality, romanticized rather than real, tinselly in the telling. Hearers may suspect that even God does not mind a good story, a harmless celebration of birth, as the first rays of the new year's sun begin to brighten the winter cold.

If we are to use the stories as a witness to God's truth, to enjoy their wealth of detail, and properly exploit their broad appeal, yet not to be shallow or merely sentimental, we need to handle them with commitment and with care, with enthusiasm and also with insight.

So this booklet tackles some linked and pointed questions. What do the gospels say about the birth of Jesus, and why do they tell it this way? How does the Christmas story fit in with the rest of the gospel story? Can honest Christians believe that Jesus was 'born of the Virgin Mary'? (I think we can.) What does Christmas tell us about God? And what can we say and celebrate this Christmas?

2   Matthew and the Tradition of Christmas

Matthew's account of Christmas, like everything else in the gospels, is like a piece of woven cloth: at every point there are threads crossing from two directions.

The gospel writers believed that certain genuine events, one particular human life, showed us the reality of God in a special way. So history and theology are meeting, and are woven together, at every point. The warp is the life of Jesus, the history that the gospel writer has to tell; and the weft is theology, the nature and purpose of God. The events of Jesus' life were important because God was at work through them, and the life and heart of God are known in fresh ways because we see them through these events. The very writing of this material is loaded with a message, and the message is accessible through the narrative. Event and meaning are bound together. The gospels are both history and theology, each of the two with its own frame and sequence, patterning one another as they cross and interweave.

Up the Family Tree

Matthew's great concern is to show Jesus against the background of the Old Testament, belonging to its history and crystallizing its hope. The opening genealogy—not everyone troubles to keep a genealogy nowadays, but first century Jews valued them highly—launches Jesus as 'the Messiah, son of David, son of Abraham' (1.1). The genealogy itself comes in three slices of fourteen generations each—beginning with Abraham, with the first section leading up to King David, and the second to the Jewish exile in Babylon, then ending up with Jesus to round off the third sequence (1.17).

These milestones themselves, the main genealogical staging posts, say something about the destination ahead. Abraham was the original Jewish patriarch, father of the chosen nation, but also the man through whose descendants the world would be blessed (Gen 12.3). To start with Abraham is to begin with a broad vision—as broad, indeed, as the view from the very end of Matthew's gospel (at 28.18–20). David was the king *par excellence*, the ancient ruler whose name had become a slogan for anointed leadership. And the exile in Babylon, the disaster of 587 BC, had never been properly undone. Never again had Israel gained strong and lasting independence in her own land. The confidence to offer light to the nations had been clouded by a saga of misfortune and subservience. Only a Messiah could change that.

So the genealogy carries coded within it a hint of royalty, a suggestion that the gloom of exile might be about to lift, and the thought that when Israel is eventually blessed the nations will be in line for blessing too. This will be a gospel for outsiders as well as insiders. As grandmother could have told you…

On the Distaff Side 1

If you look hard enough, there are five women in the genealogy: Tamar (verse 3), Rahab and Ruth (5), Bathsheba (6), and Mary (16). Leaving Mary aside for the moment, the four older women are a curious bunch. At least two, and possibly all four, were Gentiles—in a predominantly Jewish blood-line. More than this, two were prostitutes, and another had come into this family through an adulterous relationship. The God who starts with Israel is not limited to dealing with Israel alone; the horizon is worldwide. And this is no ideal and tidy genealogy, full of superstars and saints. The men, as surely as the women, are a varied company. God's purposes have taken up the tangled relationships of human life, the complications and compromises that people actually get into, to bring hope into the story and out of story. Matthew's genealogy is no smooth and sheltered heritage—which may suggest that the curious (and for some people, dubious) process by which Mary's son came to birth is quite within the pattern and purpose of God—a fulfilment of what has gone before…

Following the Formula

Matthew is keen on fulfilment. As genealogy slips into narrative, the story keeps being interrupted by quotations from the Old Testament, each one prefixed by a self-conscious formula. 'All this took place to fulfil what had been spoken by the Lord through the prophet,' introduces 1.23, and there are similar expressions at 2.6, 15, 18, and 23, linking the story that Matthew tells to figures and episodes in the Old Testament.

- 1.23 quotes Isaiah 7.14, and is used by Matthew to support his account of the Virgin Birth. Whether anyone read the original saying as referring to a extraordinary birth, we cannot now tell. What is clear is that Isaiah's prophecy anticipated the coming of an extraordinary child, a new prince, a king-to-be, in whom God's presence would be truly known. That is certainly how Matthew sees Jesus, as 'the child born king of the Jews' (2.2). So the text serves Matthew more fully than it may have served its original hearers. For him it speaks about an unusual mode of birth, as well as about a royal destiny. Yet the original thrust of the words is retained, and indeed sharpened, for Jesus will be the king of all kings, the bringer of the Kingdom of God.

- 2.6 is another royal text, from Micah 5.2–4. It speaks of a shepherd king, sent by God, and coming from Bethlehem. This was David's home town, and the hope is that once again there will be a truly anointed king, one like David, a shepherd and a ruler of the people of Israel.

- 2.15 draws on Hosea 11.1 and describes Jesus as one who re-enacts the Exodus. God's call to Israel, to come out of Egypt, is given again, and taken up in Jesus. A fresh hope of freedom is in the air. The national identity and destiny are coming to new focus in him.

- 2.18 takes up Jeremiah 31.15, and sets Herod's threat to Jesus' life, and his killing of the children of Bethlehem, against the slaughter and sorrow of the exile. Jesus has entered into Israel's grief, a grief that goes on. The harshness that characterized the exile still continues, in the rule of Herod.

- Finally 2.23, which no-one can trace. There simply is not a verse quite like this in the OT. Guesses are legion. Perhaps the best suggestion links, via a Jewish word-play, to Isaiah 11.1. This Isaiah text is again about a coming king, a 'branch' from the root of David's line. The Hebrew for 'branch' is *nezer,* and in a language based primarily on consonants that rings with the same sound as the name 'Nazareth.' It is possible that the name 'Nazareth' had come from a royal clan who settled there, so that the matching of the consonants was a deliberate echo.[2] Certainly for Matthew, Jesus, who lived at Nazareth, is the great *nezer,* the prince of hope and promise.

There are about half a dozen other fulfilment texts in Matthew, for example at 4.15f. Yet they come especially thick and fast in the birth narrative. Together they hint that the coming of Jesus can only be fully understood if he is seen as the culmination and climax of Israel's ancient hopes. He is the king who will reactivate the promise of anointed leadership. He is the one through whom Exile will pass into Exodus, frustration into freedom. He is the one through whom the nation's history will find fresh meaning, new direction. Through him God will give the chosen people a clearer sense of his presence and of their destiny. He will be the great 'Emmanuel'—which means 'God is with us' (1.23). He comes first to be with Israel, then later as Israel's life is spread out in the mission of the church, that same Emmanuel remains 'with you, always' (28.20).

Width and Wisdom

So in such a Jewish story, what are foreigners doing? Why the strange visitors, fresh from the mysterious east, laden with gifts? Matthew does not offer many clues. The wise men appear from beyond the horizon and go back to their own country. Like Melchizedek of old (Gen 14), their impact on the story seems to be enhanced by the strangeness of their coming and the secrecy of their leaving. How do they help the message? Perhaps because their story opens up two wide horizons.

- The star brings the tribute of the created order to Jesus. Not the human realm alone, but nature in all its distance and majesty is changed by his coming, and gathers to worship him. The hovering of the star (2.9) could be a messianic sign (Num 24.17). Yet in Matthew's story it is also a foil to the darkness and earthquake of the crucifixion (27.45, 51). At Jesus' birth light gathers around him; when he dies the earth and heavens groan.[3]

- The visitors bring the wealth of the Gentile world. The light of Israel rises in the coming of Jesus (Is 60.1f), and the wealth of nations converges, to add to the praise of God's glory (Is 60.3–6). The gifts laid in joyful worship around the crib are a foretaste of the pilgrim worship of the whole earth, coming to the city of God (Rev 21.26, a chapter with many echoes of Isaiah 60). The coming of the magi is a first instalment of Gentile mission, another signpost towards the wide horizon at the end of Matthew's gospel.

Liberator and Lawgiver

Yet another Old Testament connection stretches through the early chapters of Matthew. Jesus is like Moses, and the story signals this in a host of ways.

- Both were threatened at birth by the edict of an evil king, and were only providentially able to escape (Matthew 2.13–18 and Exodus 2).

- Both came out of Egypt to journey to the land of Israel (Matthew 2.15, 19–21, and the Exodus).

- Both came through water (Jesus' baptism, and Moses' crossing of the Red Sea).

- Both spent time in the wilderness (Jesus' temptation, in Matthew 4.1–11, where the texts from Deuteronomy recall Israel's desert journey).

- Finally, both went up a mountain to bring to Israel God's commands. Matthew 5, the Sermon on the Mount, is the new Sinai, Jesus' teaching place, where he gives a new and fuller law of righteousness. Much of the teaching in that section is directly set alongside the ancient Law of Moses (see the 'six antitheses' in 5.17–48).

More details have been traced from elsewhere in the gospel. The main point is that Jesus comes to Israel with a ministry as significant as that of Moses, indeed superseding and surpassing Moses. He does afresh what Moses did. He sets in motion a new covenant, a genuinely new era in God's dealings with the nation, yet an era whose story resonates with all that God has done in the past.

Christmas Past

Matthew's key theological theme is that the present, the coming of Jesus, is grounded in the past. In a host of ways the Old Testament comes to life. It finds fullness and a fresh beginning in the birth, being and activity of Jesus Christ. Jesus is a Jewish Christ, only fully understood against the background of Israel's Scripture, realizing the hopes of that Scripture, and bringing its promises to fulfilment. Christianity is grounded in Judaism, the New Testament in the Old, and the events of the gospel in the promises of the past.

Matthew's emphasis is important for Christian theology. We must link our New Testament faith to the long history of Israel. That releases for us the rich resources of the Old Testament, not simply as a dull warm-up to the real action, but as a book of promise, redolent with grace, hope and love. At the very start of the New Testament, Matthew revels in the Old.

So perhaps one of Matthew's questions to the church would be, 'What are you doing with Advent?' Do you belong to one of those churches that seems to get tunnel vision from the very start of Advent, can sing of nothing but shepherds and angels for the whole of December, and gets ever so slightly bored with celebrating Christmas before it even arrives? Or do you take advantage of Advent to show how God prepared for Christmas, and listen to the ancient Scriptures of hope, so that Christmas is a real climax, anticipated in preaching as well as in shopping? Of course there is a balance. We do not ignore the opportunities we get to tell of Jesus before December 25th. But we may rightly tell also of a God whose purpose spans history, for whom Christmas was not a total surprise.

This leads on to a broader pastoral relevance in Matthew's approach. There is a measured quality about God's purposes through time; grace is often slow and sure. The present is more than just a passing frame on the celluloid called experience; it is part of a bigger drama. Nor is the past simply a museum for visiting in nostalgic moments; its own significance is enhanced and expanded through the present to which it has led.

Celebrating Christmas—meeting relatives, travelling to the old family home, going to church together—or doing things very differently, because someone is no longer there—causes many people to engage with their own past. Old memories and landmarks come into mind, and ask to be honoured. Matthew's Christmas gospel invites us to take the past seriously, to recognize how it shapes the present, and to honour what God has done for us through it. We do not offer homage as if to a self-contained era, now inaccessible to us. But we respect the past, and thank God for it, as it has been purposeful, formative and fruitful, opening our eyes and our hearts to the experience of God that is ours today. Similarly we find in the present not just a lonely moment, but an opportunity for faith and service formed by what has gone before, and intended to reveal some of its own glory through the future which God shapes from it.

3 Luke and the Spirit of Christmas

As in Matthew, so in Luke.

History and theology are woven together. Undoubtedly Luke's preface offers a gospel based in history, and makes clear his sense of responsibility as a historian (Lk 1.1–4). But Luke is also a theologian, eager to tell of the work of God. His outlook is profoundly biblical; for him, as for Matthew, the Old Testament is brought to fulfilment in the story of Jesus.

Indeed Luke tells his whole story as a story of fulfilment. From the very beginning we read of 'the things fulfilled among us' (1.1), and at several critical turning points in Luke and Acts the language of fulfilment is used. This is more than 'took place' or 'happened'; Luke senses that an expected promise is becoming real and active. The wind of the Spirit is blowing again.

Breath of Life

Luke refers to the Holy Spirit of God more often than do any of the other gospel writers. It is in the early chapters that he points most often to the Spirit's presence and work.

There were some in Israel who thought of the Spirit's activity as rather 'rare, relatively lacking in quality and power.'[4] Yet the coming messianic age would be a time of rich spiritual blessing. The dead leaves of autumn would be rustled by the new breath of spring.

Luke tells of the coming of that hope, the arrival of the longed-for Spirit, reaching into the piety of ancient Israel, stirring young and old alike to greet the coming of God's salvation. Elizabeth and Zechariah are enabled to have a son when they are deep into middle age, and the Spirit will fill his life (1.15). The same Spirit stirs in the body of young Mary, to prompt the conception of her holy child, Jesus (1.35). These parents burst out into psalms of praise, inspired by the Spirit—Elizabeth (1.41), Mary (1.46), and Zechariah (1.67). Their praise is echoed by the midnight choir of angels (2.14), by the solemn hope of Simeon (2.29–32) and the joy of Anna (2.36–38). The reader can almost hear the patter of rain on dry ground, the whisper of breath animating dry bones, the laughter that greets the fulfilment of longing. God is moving in Israel again. The Messiah is born. His herald goes before him. This is the stuff of glad praise.

Notes of Hope

There are three glorious songs in this opening act of Luke's gospel: the *Magnificat*, which is Mary's song (1.46–55); Zechariah's *Benedictus* (1.68–79); and Simeon's *Nunc Dimittis* (2.29–32—see also 34–35).[5] All three draw heavily upon the Old Testament, gathering texts and phrases from the ancient Scripture into a collage of hope and praise. All three have a single theme: the faithfulness of God, who has brought promises to life, and who will once again do great things in Israel. Yet they have their own distinct accents and emphases.

Mary's song revels in the mercy of God, which she has received in a special way. There is a personal note within her praise (1.48f), but this is not just an individual rejoicing. She sings for the faithful, whom God has seen and blessed (1.50f). She sings for the poor, lifted up by God (1.52f). And she sings for Israel, receiving afresh the promise once made to Abraham (1.54f). Her four couplets express a single message in four different ways: what God does for Mary he does for Israel, who has waited in faith, and has often known herself to be poor in the eyes of the world. To poverty comes new wealth, to faith comes mercy, to Israel comes God—and Mary sings praise for Israel, humbly and faithfully receiving her God, who is coming to life within her.

Zechariah's song is a hymn for the nation. As befits a priest of Israel, he emphasizes much more directly than Mary the national aspect. Leadership and freedom are his themes (1.69, 71), freedom to serve God properly (1.74–75). He sings too of his son John, the herald and prophet of this hope, going ahead of the Lord to prepare the people for their light and guide (1.76–79).

Finally Simeon looks beyond Israel, at the 'light to the nations' which is beginning to shine in Jesus, at the hope which will extend to embrace the world (2.30–32). Then as we overhear the awesome and private warning to Mary, in verses 34–35, we realize that this ministry will be sharp to bear. Those who love Jesus most intimately will be hurt the most severely, and the sword of opposition will cut deep. The Messiah's leadership will cost him dear, as he reaches the Gentiles with the light of God.

Will the Real Prophet...?

Mary's song has an intriguing Old Testament connection: it is strikingly similar to Hannah's song in 1 Samuel 2.1–10. This similarity is part of an important undercurrent through the opening chapters of Luke. The most obvious clue is at Luke 2.52, which reproduces 1 Samuel 2.26. Then we see a host of contacts between the two stories—but the pattern and meaning they yield are not immediately clear.

- Hannah was like Elizabeth: she had been so long without children that she had ceased to expect them; then she gave birth to a child who would come with a prophetic message of judgment to Israel.

- Hannah was like Mary, for their songs are so similar, and their sons are spoken of in similar ways (Lk 2.52 with 1 Sam 2.26).

- Samuel was like Jesus (Luke 2.41–50), a child in the Temple, who knew God's purposes better than the clergy did (1 Sam 3).

- Samuel was like John: he launched a king into service, when he anointed David (1 Sam 16), just as John's baptism was the moment when Jesus could begin his ministry.

So the contacts are live, but the wires seem to be crossed. Is it Jesus or John who takes up the prophetic ministry of Samuel? Is Jesus modelled on Samuel the prophet or on David the king? What of the close correspondence between the birth accounts of Jesus and of John? — for they seem woven into each other, stage by stage. Are Jesus and John intentionally portrayed as two of a kind?

I think this is part of the explanation. John and Jesus are parallel figures. Both are prophets, with a message from God; in that sense both of them are like Samuel. Yet at the moment of baptism (3.21–22) Jesus is a royal figure, the anointed Son of God, and John is only a supporting actor, already on the point of leaving the stage (3.20). Jesus' ministry will stretch beyond that of John, in time, in reach, and in importance. And indeed this is foreshadowed in the infancy stories themselves. There is a parallel, but it is not sustained. There is a 'tilt' in the layout of the story, so that as it develops Jesus receives much more attention than John does.[6] His birth is heralded by angels (2.13), John's by neighbours (1.58). His childhood includes an astounding incident in the Temple (2.41–50); we hear only briefly that John was in the wilderness (1.80). By shifting the emphasis to rest progressively more heavily on Jesus, the infancy chapters point to the time when Jesus' ministry will succeed and surpass what John has done. John helps to launch the ship; Jesus sails it.

So Jesus is prophet, and more than a prophet. He is prophet and king. He comes both to tell and to lead. He comes to speak of God, and to embody the ancient hopes for an anointed saviour. The birth narrative in Luke is only really complete when Jesus stands up to teach in the synagogue, and tells the watching congregation that the Spirit of the Lord is upon him (4.16–21). Then he begins to serve, in the power of the Spirit, in the way for which he was born. Good news comes to the needy...

Forward to Reversal

'Good news to the poor' (4.18) is one of Luke's great themes—that God notices the plight and desperation of human need, that unfortunate people matter to heaven, and that many of the values, scales and hierarchies of earth look very different through the lens of the gospel. Jesus has a particular affinity with people on the margins, with the disadvantaged and disappointed. In a host of important ways the gospel is a message of reversal.

In the birth stories we overhear the first click of the divine gear-lever slipping into reversal. Mary sings of scattered pride and lowliness raised high, of hungry stomachs filled and heavy bank balances that gain no purchase with God (1.51–53). The shepherds come to worship, 'ordinary, lowly people,'[7] perhaps not especially poor but certainly not affluent or prominent folk, and their worship makes harmony with the angels' song (2.13f, 20). The Messiah takes his place among the common people, and receives their praise. Then when the child is brought to the Temple at forty days old, the sacrifice offered by his parents is 'a pair of doves' (2.24), the permitted alternative for a couple unable to afford the regular offering of a sheep (Lev 12.8).

The life of Israel is being touched from below, by a Saviour who arises from among the people, who experiences pressures and distresses of ordinary life. The world is to be turned upside-down (Acts 17.6) by the movement he launches. The birth of Jesus, as Luke tells it, is a moment laden with potential...

God Surprises

Luke knows as well as Matthew that Christmas is grounded in the past, and he expresses this in many ways. Yet his own sights are on the future. His narrative is brimming with expectancy—not just the expectancy of a birth, but the hope that looks forward from that birth and because of it. The birth is only a beginning. Luke's Christmas message is a message of promise. God's coming in Jesus releases the Spirit in our world. Things will not be the same again. There is a prospect of change in the air, life and vision are being set free. God's good news is reaching across the earth. Let a weary world rejoice.

That emphasis continues throughout Luke's story, to the end of Acts. The child whose birthplace is fixed by an imperial census (Lk 2.1–7) will be preached in an expanding circle of witness, that goes all the way back to Rome, to the source of the emperor's command. The message spreads out stage by stage, crossing racial, cultural and geographical boundaries, facing and overcoming opposition. God's gospel moves towards the ends of the earth, and at the close of Acts the story does not finish—Paul preaches 'openly and unhindered' (Acts 28.31), and the progress of the faith will stretch away to nations beyond.

So Luke's challenge to the church asks about our expectancy. We cannot copy the first Christmas; it was a unique event. Yet that event has set a renewing work of God in motion, in which we are invited to share. The same Spirit who stirred in the coming of Jesus, who rested on Jesus and activated his ministry, remains alive in the church today. God's work still draws young people like Mary and John, middle-aged people like Zechariah and Elizabeth, old people like Simeon and Anna, into possibilities of faith and service that surprise, disturb and delight them. God still works in ways that have explosive and far-reaching potential. God's horizons still extend beyond ours.

Luke's account of Christmas invites Christians to live in hope. It speaks to the young person who fears that life may lack purpose, and to the mature man or woman whose vision of God is narrowing and fading. It tells of a God who is rich in purpose, broad in perspective, dynamic in power, and utterly down-to-earth in the ways that he meets ordinary men and women.

Our Christmas seasons sometimes bring events or moments that seem to press the pause button on struggles and conflicts and selfishness. We may sense that these pauses cannot last; realism will have to prevail. Yet Luke's message is that God does the unexpected, leads us into the improbable, and goes beyond what we ask or think. The mystique of Christmas is precious, because at its best it can give a small taste of blessing ahead; it invites us to cherish that blessing even now, and to live accordingly. There is always a cost in living hopefully—Simeon's words to Mary remind us of that. Yet hopefully is the way to live. God sent Jesus into a time and place where hope was vulnerable, where thoughts of promise often seemed pale and distant. And God breathed into that time, and reached out from it to liberate, to love, and to touch the nations. We look forward now because we have looked back at the gospel story, and seen there the forward movement of God. As Luke would remind us, hope arises out of history, out of what happened in Jesus.

Mary and the History of Christmas 4

History, of course, is a big question.

Did Christmas really happen? Matthew and Luke's work is so dense in theological allusion, so richly textured with Old Testament material. The stories they tell are thoroughly unusual, in a host of ways. Are these actual events, or have theology and symbolic story taken over from sober history? Were these accounts created from the authors' imagination, to draw attention to the nature and significance of this holy child, rather than because the birth was actually like this? Can a thoughtful and honest person believe that any of this happened?

I think the answer to the last question is a clear 'Yes.' But the evidence for different elements of the Christmas story varies a good deal.[8]

Around the Crib

There is no ancient evidence, from anywhere other than the gospels, for the coming of the wise men (Mt 2.1–12), or for the shepherds' visit (Lk 2.8–20).[9]

The star of Bethlehem (Mt 2.2, 9) has attracted as much attention from modern scholars as it ever did in ancient times. Several theories have been offered, to connect it to known movements in the sky, to other ancient observations, or to regular orbits of the heavenly bodies. It is possible that a comet, also spotted in China, was the star that led the magi, and this suggestion may connect with other material from the birth stories. It would date the birth of Jesus to the spring of 5 BC.[10]

The massacre of the innocents (Mt 2.16) corresponds to the terrible paranoia of the ageing Herod, his angry fear of anyone who might be likely to succeed him, of which we read in the Jewish historian Josephus.[11] In the closing years of his life Herod killed three of his own sons, and numerous others. He might well have acted very harshly to get rid of the prince of Bethlehem.

The census (Lk 2.1–5) raises some questions. Was it for taxation purposes, or more basically a census of allegiance to the Roman Emperor, as Josephus records?[12] Quirinius (2.2) had a long and busy career, but we have no clear evidence of his being governor of Syria as early as 5 BC. It is possible that he ruled Syria in this period, or it may be that Lk 2.2 should be translated 'this was the census before Quirinius was governor of Syria.' Certainly census-taking was a significant feature of ancient government, and we have records of the practice which correspond in several ways to the information Luke gives us. Nonetheless opinion remains divided as to Luke's reliability in these details.[13]

Matthew (1.1–17) and Luke (3.23–38) offer very different versions of the genealogy of Jesus. Why do they differ? Two explanations have been offered: that one genealogy gives Joseph's line, and the other Mary's; or that one list traces biological descent, and the other the line of royal succession from David.[14] If neither of these seems plausible to us, we might reckon that the genealogies were primarily theological rather than historical in their purpose.[15]

This takes us on to the central elements of the Christmas story, the conception and birth of Jesus. And here we have more to consider, in two senses. Firstly, the way in which Jesus began his human life is a matter of great importance for Christians—as the sixth chapter of this booklet will outline. Secondly, the material itself comes from both Matthew and Luke, and in major ways they corroborate one another's stories. I cannot offer positive proof for the virgin birth. But the evidence is quite considerable.

Born of the Virgin Mary

The two accounts, in Matthew and Luke, have a great deal of common material, including the following:

> The parents, Mary and Joseph, are legally engaged, but have not yet had sexual relations. The child is conceived by the Holy Spirit, without Joseph's sexual involvement. An angel tells the parents of the coming birth, and tells them what the child is to be called. The birth takes place in Bethlehem, after the parents' marriage.

On the essential core of the story the two authors agree. Yet they are sufficiently different in a host of other details—each includes a great deal that the other misses—to suggest a substantial degree of independence.

Two very different accounts, then, speak for the virgin birth. What of their reliability?

One of the writers, Luke, begins his gospel with a high claim about careful historical investigation (1.1–4). He goes on to scatter through his early chapters precise details of the passing of time (1.24, 26, 56) and cross references to secular history (1.5, 2.1f, 3.1f). It certainly seems that he wishes his readers to take seriously what he says about the birth of Jesus. Further, his credentials as a historian stand up pretty well at a variety of places in the gospel and Acts where they are amenable to cross-checking; what he says at the start of his gospel is not mere bluff.

The other witness, Matthew, is keen to show that the Christian story is a ful-filment of prophecies in the Old Testament. Yet when he writes of the virgin birth he invokes an OT text, Isaiah 7.14, that had not previously been used to predict a virgin-born Messiah. Expectation of a virgin birth was not part of the Jewish background; it did not figure in their identikit for the Messiah. It seems, then, that the Isaiah text is used by Matthew because it fits the facts that he has to tell. Matthew's account of the virgin birth has not been shaped by a prior agenda, but by the event itself.

Obviously Luke and Matthew vary considerably—even though many scholars reckon the two stories compatible. But it is at the heart of the story that these two evangelists are closest, and here that both of them—I argue—should be heeded as responsible witnesses.

Beside the direct accounts in Matthew and Luke, several other NT texts may suggest in passing that their writers knew of the virgin birth, and of the counter charge from outside the church that Jesus was illegitimate. These texts include Mark 6.3, John 8.41, and Galatians 4.4.[16] And if there is silence in other places in the NT, that may be because the early Christians were cau-tious about throwaway references to the virgin birth; they wanted to avoid misunderstanding in a society acquainted with extravagant pagan legends.

This leads us to one historical objection that has been raised. There are various stories from the ancient Mediterranean world about the births of prominent leaders, sometimes involving the union of a god and a human woman. Could the Christian story about the birth of Jesus have been influenced by these?

Probably not, is the answer. There is certainly no evidence of any connection, and the parallels are not close. By and large these Greco-Roman traditions are more colourful, and more overtly sexual, in their detail. The gospel accounts of the virgin birth show a proper restraint and reverence in the presence of God's action.[17] Indeed it would be odd if sections of the NT as thoroughly Jewish in atmosphere and tone as the early chapters of Matthew and Luke, had been influenced by stories and traditions quite alien to the Jewish belief in the holiness and transcendence of God.

Of course God's dealings with Mary are mysterious; this is not the sort of biblical event for which we should expect a cloud of witnesses, nor a mass of detail. There is a proper privacy about conception; there is bound to be mystery in the incarnation of God. Yet we have enough to believe, not against the evidence, but because of it, that Jesus was conceived by the Holy Ghost and born of the Virgin Mary. What we celebrate at Christmas need not be dismissed as an ancient fiction, but may be welcomed and worshipped as the gentle and decisive coming of God, by the gracious action of the Holy Spirit, into the receptive and loving care of a young Jewish mother.

5 John and the Glory of Christmas

John's Christmas story is both shorter and longer than Matthew's and Luke's—shorter, in that it finishes in eighteen verses; longer because it reaches further back, to start 'in the beginning' (1.1).

God's word comes, the creative voice that made the world. Yet the narrative holds a kind of suspense: it is not obvious that the word is a person until v 10,[18] only in v 14 do we have the dramatic statement that 'the word became flesh,' and and he is not named as Jesus until v 17. The broad expanse of eternity focuses down to the human coming of Jesus Christ. Yet even in the narrowing focus, majesty and glory shine through, so that a world which never saw God suddenly finds him visible and known. John's prologue offers drama rather than description, the significance rather than the story, of the coming of Jesus.

Creative Word (vv 1–5)

The opening verses parallel the initial paragraphs of Genesis. The very first words give a precise echo of the start of creation, 'in the beginning.' Then come word and life, light and darkness. The language is cast in deliberate recall of Israel's Scripture, the event itself is momentous as creation. The word becomes flesh within the heritage and faith of the Jewish people, yet for the whole world, that the whole of creation may be touched afresh with the life of God who formed it.

Historical Word (vv 6–9)

Coming from the beginning, from the boundaries of light and darkness, giver of the life of all humanity, the word is heard, and the light seen, in a particular time and place, within range of John's witness, in Israel, in the opening decades of the first century. The word is located, the light gleams into history; this is the point of entry.

Rejected Word (vv 10-11)

There is a world between coming and welcoming. The word is not received kindly in the world he made. Israel, 'his own people,' do not accept him. In this they are no better and no worse than the rest of the world that 'did not know him.' They are the particular nation in whom the whole drama of God's dealings with humanity is played out, on a smaller stage but with a similar plot. So the work of his coming, the fruit of the incarnation, will be the forming of a new people, to lead the world back to God.

Birthing Word (vv 12-14)

For those who do receive the word, a people gathered first from Israel and then later from further afield, a new relationship is brought into being: they become children of God. That is not a biological or genetic bond. It does not happen by 'blood,' by human descent, nor by 'the desire of the flesh or of a man.' It transcends all that, and is brought into being 'of God.' Spiritual life does not come from physical birth. In that sense flesh and spirit are independent. But human flesh, the flesh taken by the eternal word, can reveal grace, truth and glory—the love, solidity and splendour of God. There flesh and spirit are linked. For himself, God can take a very particular piece of human flesh, and make himself known through and within it. For us, God can give life in ways that transcend our physical makeup, our communal bonds, and our genetic identity.

That is how these verses read—with one intriguing query. Some ancient copies or discussions of John's gospel offer a different version of verse 13, with 'was born' instead of 'were born.' This switch into the singular—and it might have been the singular that John wrote—implies that v 13 is about 'him,' about the word, the light, the one who came. It speaks of his becoming flesh, in a way that did not depend on 'blood, human desire, or a husband's will.' So possibly John knew of the virgin birth; indeed, even if the plural 'were born' is what John wrote, he might still be alluding to the mysterious birth of Jesus, as a precedent for the new birth of Christians by the direct action of God. If John knew about the virgin birth, there might be other allusions too, for example in 6.42 and 8.41. What did John write at 1.13, and what did he mean? Like much in history, we cannot be sure.

Direct Word (vv 15-18)

This final part of John's prologue portrays Jesus as successor to Moses. There are recollections of Moses' encounter with God in Exodus 33 and 34: 'glory' (33.18); 'no-one shall see God' (33.20); 'grace and truth (steadfast love and faithfulness)' (34.6). The law was given to and through Moses, accompanied by just a glimpse of the afterglow of God's passing. Jesus came as God's new word—not delivered through a messenger, but message incarnate—and revealed the glory of God with an unprecedented immediacy and intimacy.

Majesty Amid Mediocrity

So as John tells of the coming of Jesus, the message is of new creation, new life, a new vision of God's glory, and a new leadership for God's people. The men and women who read John's gospel are beckoned to become children of God, sons and daughters of the new realm, witnesses to God's love for the world he made. And this new realm is brought in by the coming of the word, Jesus Christ, in whom the glory of God shared our human flesh.

If Matthew's perspective on Christmas values the past, and Luke helps us to look to the future, then John speaks to the greyness of our present. Many people travel through the long stretches of middle life. Excitement is an old memory; rest a distant oasis—or mirage. In between the road is rugged and dull. Life is easily seen in shades of grey. Every silver lining has a cloud. Every decision seems to be a compromise. People seem harder to trust than once we thought. And the question arises, Is there any word of truth, any light you can steer by, anyone you can really look up to? Is humanity a thing of glory—or is it just grey?

John's message offers an answer. 'We beheld his glory.' Jesus is a word from outside—truth from God, light of a different purity, life in all its fullness. In him is the glory of real human living. He lives and calls and beckons. And he promises to transform and use our frail lives to serve his purpose and bring glory to those around us.

Jesus and the Doctrine of Christmas[19]

6

Linking the New Testament material on Christmas to the rest of Christian belief involves two important ideas, closely connected but not identical: incarnation and virgin birth.

Flesh of Our Flesh

To talk of incarnation implies the en-fleshing of God, the coming of the Son of God in the humanity of Jesus. The incarnation means that the one who was born at Bethlehem was the eternal Son of God. In origin he was divine; in eternity God was his Father. He did not begin at Bethlehem, but, 'In the beginning was the Word, and the Word was with God, and the Word was God' (Jn 1.1).

The incarnation takes a pivotal role in Christian faith. If Jesus of Nazareth was more than merely a man, if God was personally present in Christ, then the cross is God's own loving, saving and reconciling act, Easter is God's own triumph over human death, we can speak of the man Jesus as reigning Lord and coming Judge, and companionship with Jesus is possible for people who reach out to him in faith. There is a personal link between our human condition and the wisdom and love, the heart and mind, of God. Without the incarnation, if Jesus of Nazareth had been just a good and godly man, we should have a rather thinner set of beliefs, and following Jesus would be more like tracing the distant steps of a figure from the past, rather than walking with a present Lord. The incarnation makes a real difference to our faith.

Son of Mary, Stepson of Joseph

The virgin birth means that the human child Jesus was conceived by the activity of the Holy Spirit, in the body of Mary his mother, without the physical involvement of a human father. Jesus was born to a woman who had never slept with a man. Legally Joseph was Jesus' father, but biologically he was not. 'Joseph, son of David, do not be afraid to take Mary as your wife, for the child conceived in her is from the Holy Spirit' (Matthew 1.20; see also Luke 1.35).

The central point is not that the child was born to a virgin mother, although Mary's virginity clearly served as sign of an unusual birth. It is Jesus' conception by the Holy Spirit that makes him who he is. So we need not believe that Mary remained virgin for the rest of her life, although some Christians do believe this.

Nor does the virgin birth imply that sex is intrinsically unholy, that it was something unworthy of God's Christ. The point is not that the Holy Spirit needed to short-circuit human sexuality in order to produce a holy child. But neither should we think that there was some kind of sexual union between God and Mary. The Holy Spirit came to Mary as creator, not as sexual partner.

So how do incarnation and virgin birth belong together?

Two Doctrines, One Reality

The virgin birth was the means by which incarnation came about. The incarnation means that Jesus of Nazareth was divine, heavenly, eternal in origin. The virgin birth means that in his becoming flesh, he had no human father. The incarnation says who and where: who he was and where he came from. The virgin birth says how: how he came among us. Incarnation is 'the word became flesh' (Jn 1.14). The virgin birth tells how he became flesh: conceived by the Holy Spirit, and born of a virgin mother.

Could it have been otherwise? Could God have become incarnate without a virgin birth? We have no clear biblical guidance and can scarcely speculate. But two gospels see a close relationship between how Jesus was born and who he was. The manner of his coming matches what he did. In Matthew Jesus is Emmanuel (God with us); the presence of God in Jesus, and his mission as Saviour, are explained by his virgin birth (1.20–23). For Luke, Jesus is holy and Son of God, because of his conception by the Spirit of God (1.35). The identity, mission, and saving work of Jesus accord with the way that he entered our world. They arise from the special role taken by the Holy Spirit in his conception and birth. He is both truly God and truly one of us.

Maker and Made

So Jesus is both created and Creator. His coming is an act of new creation, yet firmly implanted in the continuing processes of the old creation. God enters his creation and becomes one with his creatures. Jesus was both like us and unlike us: one of the human race, yet inaugurating a new humanity; a created person, yet one in whom a new creation finds its life and identity.

As a creative act of God, the virgin birth is like the resurrection. These have been called the two great miracles of the gospels. They come at the beginning and end of Jesus' earthly life. In contrast to the other miracles, they were not done by Jesus, but rather they were done in him and to him. Both are about life taking shape—in the womb, and in the tomb. The resurrection makes visible to others and available for sharing, what is private and individual in the birth—that in sheer mystery, beyond our power to analyse or explain, God can bring life where we did not expect it.

7

Theologians and Reflection on Christmas

The Christmas material has given rich opportunity for some very varied theological reflection, through nearly two thousand years.

Here are a few samples—by no means a survey, just a small collection.

Christmas and Creation

Some of the earliest reflection on the coming of Jesus, from the second century, thought of the relationship of this event to the created order. One text stresses the sheer secrecy and mystery of the event, 'hidden from the heavens, from the princes, from the gods of this world.'[20] Other writers were attracted, like the magi, to the star: it is superior to any other, inspiring awe and fear among the other stars, and ending the domination of astral powers over human life.[21] We hear too of Jesus' baptism making holy the waters of chaos; the disorder and threat of the watery realm is touched by the sanctifying presence of the Son of God.[22]

There is a sense on the one hand of something inscrutable, that the created order can neither observe nor resist. Alongside this is a sense that the natural order itself has its sting drawn, so that neither the skies above nor the waters beneath retain their ancient power to harm. We know—and so did those early Christian writers—that things are not quite as simple as this: nature is still a dangerous and ambiguous realm. Yet Christmas interrupts this pattern, and points to its ultimate dissolution, with the coming of incarnate goodness.

Christmas and Gender

Christian theologians in the fourth century wrote on the virgin state in which Mary gave birth. God was treating the feminine side of humanity as honourable and holy, releasing the daughters of Eve from the memory of the fall, removing that stigma and the bitterness it brought.[23]

In modern times, freshly aware of gender issues, theologians have returned to similar themes. The virgin birth shows God's salvation by-passing patriarchy. Woman has an integrity in herself, independent here of any male domination or partnership. She is the one who bears the divine presence. Indeed Mary's submission to God—'I am the handmaid of the Lord. Let it be to me according to your word' (Lk 1.38)—marks God's working through the receptive (typically feminine) side of human life, without the involvement of powerful and determined masculinity.[24]

Some Christians look to Mary in their prayers, and others reckon that a role she should not be asked to take. But undoubtedly she speaks to us from the pages of the New Testament as a model of obedience, receptive to the work of God, seeking only to be faithful in the role chosen for her. In that she is a distinctive example to us all.

Christmas and Poverty

Liberation theologians, keen to trace God's working in places of oppression and suffering, have found ready inspiration in the Christmas narrative. Through this child God identifies himself with troubled humanity: with a subject people, among whom he came; with homeless families and with communities who lack decent health care by his birth in an animals' stall; with the refugees of the world, for he fled helpless to Egypt; and with the vulnerable, poor and persecuted of every land.

It is admittedly difficult to know the exact socioeconomic status of the home in Nazareth where Jesus grew up. But the birth narratives indicate that his family were no strangers to the harshness of human existence. When Jesus said, 'Blessed are you poor' (Lk 6.20), this poverty had come very close to home.

8 Preachers and Christmas

Preaching the Christmas story is one of the greatest opportunities given to any leader of Christian worship.

To excite a congregation with the message of God's commitment to our humanity, to share with both regular and occasional worshippers the mystery and the sheer ordinariness of the Christ child—this is a privilege indeed. So what can a biblical study booklet say about preaching Christmas?

The Gospel Before Us

Be selective in what you preach. Use the particular gospel from which you read in your service. For example, if your reading is from Matthew, you can speak gladly of Jesus as the fulfilment of God's purpose, the heart and focus of an ancient divine plan; you can tell of a God who works through time, and whose work is centred on Jesus. But if you want to speak of the stirring of God's Spirit, the God of the unexpected, then Luke will serve you better. If you want to speak of the Christ who came to give people new life, then John's prologue can help you. Jesus coming to communicate is a Johannine theme—'the word'; Jesus the liberator flows better from Luke; Jesus the king is a Matthean emphasis, and so on. Let your Scripture speak through your preaching. Use the themes you read (or, if your lectionary allows, read the themes you mean to use).

The People Before Us

Every preaching has a context, a people to whom it is delivered, with their own joys, pressures and griefs, some of these shared by the whole company and some very individual. Preach to the people there. Christmas presents so many themes; you can afford to choose. What will this congregation be able to hear? What will help them, what will consolidate them in the faith they hold, or move them on to deeper knowledge of God? What will stir, what will soothe, what will meet their needs, and what will miss? Christmas always gives you so many choices. And do be imaginative with illustration; a message about incarnation deserves to be illustrated from people's experience. Use the opportunities of the place and the moment. Here are two actual stories that began talks in evangelistic carol services, at a science lab and at a football club, one recalling a visit to a school, the other from a footballer turned vicar.[24]

1) 'The science block was a crumbling wartime hut; a dull, discouraging, depressing sight. Yet inside it was full of energy and imagination, a place where any youngster was liable to become hooked on science. You might have guessed it would be like this, if you read the card pinned to the outside door: "Do not judge us by our appearances. Remember Crick and Watson discovered DNA in a bicycle shed." The stuff of which life is made, discovered in a shed; and the Maker of life was born in one. If a shed may be a place of wonder and discovery, then take time to discover what was going on in the shed at Bethlehem...'

2) 'As a boy I watched football on the TV, and my idol was the great Dutch player of the '70s, Johan Cruyff. I tried to copy him when I played with my friends; but he and I were in different leagues. Then, at the very beginning of my footballing career, and at the very end of his, I found myself playing on the same pitch as Johan Cruyff.' What a beginning for a sermon on Christmas!—the God known only from afar came to our turf, to share our struggle and play the game of life with us...

Examples only. Christmas is about God with us. The message itself surely invites us to find ways of telling the good news accessibly to the people who hear, that they may know God with them.

Notes

1 The issues of this paragraph are discussed in M D Hooker, *Beginnings* (London: SCM, 1997) pp 27f—an admirable, concise and accessible exposition of the openings of all four gospels.

2 B Pixner, *With Jesus through Galilee According to the Fifth Gospel* (Israel: Corazin, 1992) pp 14–19.

3 An unpublished piece by David Dones helped me to see this connection.

4 Max Turner, *The Holy Spirit and Spiritual Gifts* (Exeter: Paternoster, 1996) p 12.

5 The Latin names of these songs come from their opening words. Benedictus means 'blessed' (1.68), and so on.

6 The term 'tilt' comes from S Farris, *The Hymns of Luke's Infancy Narrative* (Sheffield, 1982).

7 I H Marshall, *The Gospel of Luke (NIGTC)* (Exeter: Paternoster, 1978) p 108.

8   This section adapts and reuses some material I wrote for *The Faith we Hold*, a collection of essays on Christian doctrines published by GEAR in the United Reformed Church, 1993.

9   There are, however, traces of a medieval Persian tradition that the magi came from Saveh in Iran. I came across this in William Dalrymple, *In Xanadu* (London: Collins, 1989).

10 C J Humphreys, 'The Star of Bethlehem, a Comet in 5 BC and the Date of Christ's Birth,' in *Tyndale Bulletin* 43 (1992) pp 31–56.

11 Josephus, *Antiquities of the Jews*, XVI.17–XVII.7.

12 See Humphreys (note above) p 50.

13 A positive assessment of Luke's account of the census issue comes in E Stauffer, *Jesus and His Story* (London: SCM, 1960) pp 27–36, and a more sceptical appraisal in R E Brown, *The Birth of the Messiah* (New York: Doubleday, 1977) pp 547–556.

14 An account of these two theories, particularly of the second, is given in pp 62–65 of D A Carson's commentary on Matthew, in F E Gaebelein(ed), *Expositor's Bible Commentary*, Vol 8 (Grand Rapids: Zondervan, 1984) pp 1–599.

15 This is the line taken by Brown, *Birth of the Messiah* (note above) pp 57–95.

16 There are others too; some of the texts are discussed in fuller detail by C E B Cranfield, 'Some Reflections on the Subject of the Virgin Birth,' in *Scottish Journal of Theology* 41 (1988) pp 177–89.

17 For a fuller discussion of this point see R E Brown, *The Virginal Conception and Bodily Resurrection of Jesus* (London: Chapman, 1973) p 62.

18 The famous (and almost the first) English translation, by William Tyndale, has 'it' in verses 3 and 4, where our modern versions read 'he.' The original Greek of the New Testament can support either.

19 This section also uses material from *The Faith we Hold* (GEAR in the URC, 1993); see note 8 above.

20 The Ascension of Isaiah, Chapters 10 and 11.

21 Ignatius to the Ephesians, Chapter 19.

22 Testament of Asher 7.3; Ignatius to the Ephesians 18.2. Much in this paragraph comes from J Daniélou, *The Theology of Jewish Christianity* (London: DLT, 1964) Chapter 7.

23 Gregory Nazianzen, *In Praise of Virginity*, drawn from V E F Harrison, 'Gender, Generation and Virginity in Cappadocian Theology,' *Journal of Theological Studies* 47.1 (1996) pp 38–68.

24 This last point is made clearly by Karl Barth, *Dogmatics in Outline* (SCM: London, 1949) pp 99f.

25 I am grateful to the Rev'd Alan Comfort for permission to use the second story.